Right Motives,

Teaching with Poverty in Mind!

Please go to AMAZON and write a review!

Every now and then, you come across an individual who lives a humble life. Yet, his very presence strikes a chord within you. Craig's story is one that moves, touches and inspires audiences. It's a story about determination and personal accountability. It's a story about a young man who refused to accept his current situation.

Although Craig has risen to high levels of success as an acclaimed author and professional speaker, it's his down-to-earth personality that endears him to those that come across his path. His message is very simple... Change Is Possible!

When Craig speaks, he reaches the hearts of his audience to motivate change in themselves and their community. Craig has devoted his life to creating lasting change for those who desire it; Craig has risen to the national stage by delivering an inspirational message which tells people how to shake off mediocrity and live up to their greatness.

It is a message that Craig has learned from his own life challenges and one he is helping others apply to their lives. Craig's personal mission in life is to provide hope to individuals who feel that their current situation is hopeless. Craig travels the country presenting his seminars and workshops. Craig has published five books since 2013 and he has been featured on talk shows, won various awards, and his story has been shared in many inspirational magazines and across the web.

My Story

At the age of 13, in 1978, my mother left New York. The move due to an altercation between her and my grandmother led my mom to Montgomery, Alabama. The story is my mother refused to obey the rules laid out by my grandmother. Around the age of 15, she met my father and shortly after became pregnant. After discovering that she

was pregnant. My mother informed my father of her condition. Frightened and uncertain as to what to do, my father, decided to abandon all responsibilities and joined the military.

Growing up with an absent parent can instill a deep sense of loss and shame in kids, especially when the absence appears to be voluntary. For some kids, abandonment extends beyond a parent's failure to support the child financially, and includes the failure to communicate with the child or play an active role in the child's life. Sadly, parental abandonment, and its effects, often leaves children with lingering questions about their own self-worth.

When I was two, I had to spend sometime in the hospital with a severe case of pneumonia. My case was so severe that the doctors didn't believe that I would survive overnight.

My tongue was swollen to the point that I couldn't swallow. Fortunately, after numerous nights in the hospital, I pulled through and survived. I lived with my grandparents for a large part of my infant and toddler days. As I understand, there were conversations of my grandparents adopting me at one point, but it never happened. My mother was in and out. Occasionally I would see her, but I guess she was off living her life.

When I was three my mother married my stepfather. My mother would ultimately become impregnated with her second child, my brother. My mother and stepfather were social drinkers. The drinking would often lead to physical altercations between the two. As a young child, I often witnessed my mother being abused by my stepfather. One particular evening my stepfather, mother and a couple of their friends were playing cards, when I witnessed my stepfather giving my younger brother a sip of alcohol from his cup.

My stepfather continued to do this over and over until my younger brother eventually stumbled and passed out. When he passed out, the adults in the room begin laughing. One day after another altercation between the two. They started fighting, my stepfather lifted my mother over his head and slammed her to the ground. During the malicious beating, my younger brother ran in the kitchen and picked up a knife and stabbed my stepfather in the back. Time went on, and the beatings and arguments became worse. In the following years my mother eventually became impregnated with my sister. I guess by this time my mom was exhausted and weary from all the fighting. After my sister was born my mother and stepfather decided to separate and eventually divorced.

What is very destructive psychologically for children is for them to experience their parents' continuing, unresolved, hostile conflicts. Research indicates that children are resilient and highly adaptive in general and can usually cope with and adapt to difficult situations such as separation and divorce. What severely damages children emotionally are bitter, long-lasting, ongoing conflicts between parents, whether the parents live together or not.

The longer parental conflict continues and the greater the tension between the parents, the greater the likelihood that psychological difficulties will result for children such as emotional and behavior problems, anxiety, depression, sleep problems, low self-esteem, difficulties in school and a number of other difficulties.

After the divorce, my mother started spending a lot of time with her then best friend. She had a younger daughter that was around the same age as me. Her daughter and I became very close friends.

Whenever they would go out partying sometime we would be left home alone. It wasn't long before sexual curiosity kicked in. Neither one of our mothers used much discretion while dealing with men. We were exposed to a great deal of things that a young child undoubtedly shouldn't see. Eventually we started experimenting and exploring each other's sexual nature. This went on for a while.

One night, while the adults were partying. We assembled as many trash cans as we could and put them in a circle behind the apartment. Once the trash cans were in place, we undressed and laid on top of one another.

She and I had no idea what it was that we were doing. After a couple minutes of engaging in these activities, our parents became curious, I guess we were too quiet. Once outside they noticed the trash cans and begin to remove them. Once removed, they found us with all our clothes off, lying on one another. Her mother took her home, my mother brought me inside of the house and made me take off all my clothes. After removing my clothes, I was placed in the bathtub.

After a few minutes in the tub, my mother pulled me out and had four of her male friends hold me down on the bed, while she pulled out an extension cord and begin whipping me. The pain was so unbearable that I began twisting and turning, trying to free my arms and legs.

I eventually broke free, but my mother continued swinging and with one power swing, she unintentionally hit me across my male private part and blood splattered all over the walls, in the bed, and on the floors. My mother was terrified; she immediately put me back in the bathtub, in an attempt to get the bleeding to stop. Eventually, the bleeding ceased, but I was never taken to the hospital for any type of evaluation.

Poverty affects the development and educational outcomes beginning in the earliest years of an individual's life, both directly and indirectly through mediated, moderated, and transactional processes. Educational readiness, or an individual's ability to use and profit from an education, has been recognized as playing a unique role in escaping from poverties grip in the United States. It is a critical element but needs to be supported by many other components of a poverty alleviation strategy, such an improved opportunity structures and empowerment of families.

Third grade, my siblings and I attended Forest Avenue Elementary School. Routinely after school, we came home and would put down our bags and go back to the school's playground until the streetlights came on. I barely remember doing any homework. If Forest Avenue had any issues they would reluctantly call my mother because she had a reputation for coming up there and getting into it with the teachers and administrators.

It took a while for me to fully understand why my mother would make us go to the park and play after school. Eventually, I begin noticing certain things. One day I came home and found her in the living room with a white couple that looked very similar to hippies. They wore bell bottoms and very bright clothes with long hair as well.

Children who grow up in an environment of illicit drug use may first see their parents using drugs. This may put them at a higher risk for developing an addiction later in life for both environmental and genetic reasons. Alcoholism and other drug addictions tend to run in families. Children of addicted parents are more at risk for alcoholism and other drug abuse than are other children.

My mother would often send us to the backroom and close the doors while she did drugs. This became normal. It was so many random people in an out of 1902 S. Hall Street. It seemed as if our house became the neighborhood hangout spot for all the local drunks and addicts in the neighborhood. I would often find medication bottles with holes punched in the side and foil covering the top (homemade crack pipes).

Many people think that crack smells like plastic. Sometimes it may have no scent at all. Also, the smell can be attributed to the products the crack is cut with, such as baking soda or ether.

Every time I discovered a crack pipe, I would take it and either put it in my backpack and take it to school, or I would flush it down the toilet. Eventually my mother caught on to what I was doing, and I would often get into trouble for moving them.

The situation at home was very difficult, but to me it was normal. We lived in a one-bedroom shotgun home. A "shotgun house" is a narrow rectangular domestic residence, usually no more than 12 feet wide, with rooms arranged one behind the other and doors at each end of the house.

As If the situation wasn't difficult enough, there were uncountable times when the food ran out before the next month. One evening I opened the refrigerator roaches scattering everywhere. Unmoved by that, I still made the sandwich.

Roaches were in the kitchen cabinets, beds, and even my clothes. I had to shake my clothes in the morning before putting them on. One school day, I went to open my backpack and numerous roaches ran out. This was one of the most embarrassing moments of my life. I tried to play it off like it wasn't me. However, another student saw it happen and the other kids joked on me the rest of the school year.

The condition of the one and only bathroom in the house was so awful. It was so nasty that I hated to use it. I usually only bathe on the weekends at my grandmother's house. As I look back, there were numerous things that I didn't learn as a child for whatever reason. I didn't start brushing my teeth until I was 14 in middle school.

One school night, around midnight, there was a loud scream coming from the living room. I jumped out of bed, along with my younger brother, and ran to see what was taking place. What we found was a man with his knee in my mother's chest ripping of her clothes.

They were drinking and using drugs. He decided that he wanted something from my mother, she refused. My brother ran in the kitchen and grabbed a knife; I picked up a lamp off the table and we both threatened the man to leave our mother alone. He eventually got up and left. That night was difficult for me, I recall lying in bed shaking, still terrified by the events that had just transpired.

Educators always express how at-risk kids miss too many days from school. I need them understand why. When you are in an at-risk situation, most of the time, getting yourself ready for school can be a challenge however now add on top of that you have to get your siblings ready as well. Makes for some frustrating morning as a kid.

One day for whatever reason I woke up late and we didn't attend school. A few hours later, a random guy came and picked us up in his vehicle. We got in the car and he drove to Burger King. My mother exited the car and went inside. As soon as she exited the vehicle, the man turned around and looked at me in the backset. He begins to drill me about not going to school that day. Then he pulled a knife out his pocket, leaned over the backseat, where I was, and stuck the knife to my throat.

The man told me, that "he would kill me, if I ever stayed my butt out of school again." Crying and frightened no one said a word. We rode around with that man, all day. My mother didn't know what had happened until I told her when we got back home, hours later. My mother called my stepfather and he rushed over. I explained what happen over and over again. He and a few of his friends left in his car looking for the gentleman. I never saw him again. It seemed that my mother's drugs habit begun to get worse.

I recall walking to the corner store to buy some eggs for my mother. The corner store sold eggs for ten cents each. She would send me to the corner store with a one-dollar food stamp (this was before EBT cards) and have me purchase a ten-cent egg and receive ninety cents in change back. If someone did this enough times they will eventually have enough change (money) to buy some cigarettes, alcohol, or even drugs. She would continue to send me to the store until she had enough change to buy whatever she desired.

Getting ready for bed one evening my mother came to me and said, "Craig I am going out tonight, Tag (a guy that hung around my mother's house) is going to watch yall tonight." I had a look of concern on my face. Tag was someone I knew; he would hang around, drink, smoke, and party with my mother but never kept us before. My siblings and I got into the bed not thinking much about the situation. We could hear Tag and the all the other guys drinking and making a lot of commotion on the porch as we lay in the bed. The next morning, as we got up to get ready for school; I walked in the living room and my mother wasn't there.

After searching the house, I began to notice that certain things were missing. The television, the microwave, food out the refrigerator, the iron, and just random things throughout the house. Afraid and not knowing what to do, I helped my brother and sister put on their clothes. We walked to the corner store and called my grandmother. She immediately came and picked us up.

Confused and unware as to how to express my frustrations, I begin to act out in school. My grades began to suffer very badly. School became less and less significant to me. My experiences in school started becoming very unpleasant. The other kids picked on me because my eyes were crossed. Many times, I'd wear the same clothes two or three times a week. I rarely bathed and often went to school with a body odor. I was involved in a lot of altercations with other students.

In third grade, the teachers and counselors became increasingly concerned about my behavior and the lack of educational motivation. During one six-week marking period, I made all F's on my report card. It was evident at this point that I had given up academically.

I am assuming that when a student is struggling the way I was; it was protocol to have him tested. The results of the test noted that I had a learning disability. With this information, the school informed my mother that they were placing me in Special Education classes. My brother would also go through the same process years later and be placed in the same curriculum with a learning disability.

Students, especially those attending high-poverty urban schools with large student bodies, primarily made up of minority students continue to be the under-performers of the U.S. educational system. Many of these students fall far behind the achievement levels of their peers in more advantaged U.S. neighborhoods or in other countries. Clear signs of behavioral and emotional disengagement from school are displayed at early ages.

I was the student that would make fun of the students in Special Education. Now I'm being placed in the same class. I felt as if other students would embarrass me the same way. Special education and students with learning disabilities are often deemed as stupid by their peers. Unfortunately, I ended up repeating the third and fifth grades.

The situation in school became so serve that the school's administration would suspend me and ask me to walk home during the middle of the school day. This was against the rules and regulations. However, the school was fed. up If something unfortunate would have happened to me walking home the school would have been liable. In most cases when I was suspended from school and walked home my mother would still be in bed. Either she would tell me to go in my room or I would have to sit in the backyard until my siblings got home.

African American males challenge educators in many ways. Perhaps the single most important challenge that has garnered recent attention in research reports, policy documents, and public commentary has been the increasing disparity in the educational achievement of African American males' relative to their peers. Although other issues, such as the need to develop programs that promote school readiness, improving teacher education, and providing resources to meet increasing academic standards, are important, the implications for achievement differentials are even more far-reaching.

The negative consequences of the achievement gap are more acute for African American males who are victimized by chronic, systemic levels of poor performance and behavior problems in school. In short, the potential loss of resources intellectual, cultural, and economic resulting from lower achievement reduces the capacity of African contributing members of their communities.

The summer was coming to an end and I was exceptionally excited. I was one year away from middle school. The first day of class I met Ms. Gaston.

Ms. Gaston was a recent college grad and we instantly connected. Ms. Gaston sat my desk next to her desk. She was the first educator that took time with me. That expressed an interest in me beyond education.

One afternoon while playing on the school playground. It began to storm. As we started walking home, a grey Honda Accord pulled up beside us. It was Ms. Gaston. She asked if she could give us a ride home. I said no thank you. She insisted.

The last day of my sixth-grade year, Ms. Gaston asked me to stay back after school was over. She leaned over and told me that she believed in me, and that my situation did not have to dictate my future. Ms. Gaston told me that either I would work hard now (in school) or I will work hard for the rest of my life." Her words hit home. This was the first time in my life that I truly felt special.

By the time I made it to junior high school things had begun to get a little better at home. My mom met a really nice guy. They would eventually get

married. In middle school I played football, basketball, and ran track. I was pretty good at it. Sports became an outlet. It was also motivation to stay out of trouble.

In most cases, getting into trouble resulted in me being sent to my football coach. That got old fast. He would make me do push-ups and run until I couldn't talk.

I was sitting in the lunchroom during 4th period my 9th grade year. I remember it like it was yesterday because I often ask myself what if I would have given my brother the keys to my car.

My brother approached me one morning and asked me if he could see the keys to my car, (I was driving a car to school in the 9th grade); for whatever reason, I told my brother no. He gave me a look as if I had just sentenced him to death. Around fourth period the same day, someone came and told me that my brother was in the office getting arrested.

I was in the lunchroom eating lunch. I franticly ran to the office, they finally informed me what happened. My brother had taken my grandmother's handgun from her house and given it to his friend. A couple of days later, his friend brought the gun back and gave it to my brother.

That day, the police took my brother and his friend to the department of youth services. They were kicked out of Montgomery Public Schools and asked to never return. This was the first time he would be incarcerated, but it wouldn't be his last. Kicked out of school, my brother begins getting into major trouble. He begins engaging in gang activity and associating with some very dangerous individuals.

He was in and out of boot camps for various reasons. He started stealing, robbing and selling drugs. He ultimately ended up in prison when he was 17, got out at 20 and went back within six months for seven more years.

A black male born in 1991 has a 29% chance of spending time in prison at some point in his life. Nearly one in three African American males aged 20–29 are under some form of criminal justice supervision whether imprisoned, jailed, on parole or probation. One out of nine African American men will be incarcerated between the ages of 20 and 34. Black males ages 30 to 34 have the highest incarceration rate of any race/ethnicity. During my middle school days, I was considered one of the top athletes in the school.

In ninth grade our football team won the city championship and I was voted all-city (which means I was one of the best at my position in the entire city of Montgomery, Alabama). My basketball team was very successful that year as well. After basketball season was over, I received a phone call from the head basketball coach at a Catholic High School. The coach met with my mother and told her that he wanted to give me a scholarship to come and play basketball for him.

The summer before, I attended Catholic High School, I began dating a young lady. No one in my family, or any of my friends were too fond of her One day while visiting her mother's house, a young man came to the door and he asked to speak to her. When she stepped outside, I went behind her.

After a brief altercation (she and I had been dating for some time. She was also cheating with him) between the two of us, he pulled out a gun and pointed at me. A few months later the young lady informed me that she was pregnant. Concerned and frightened, I didn't know what to do, because I felt like I was repeating the cycle of my mother and father. After telling my mother and seeing her disappointment, I decided to do the notable thing and began to do what I could to help her with the situation that we had created. I would leave school early for doctor appointments. I began saving money, knowing that a baby would be expensive.

One day as her sister and I were returning from shopping for baby beds, her younger sister came out and told me that her sisters baby wasn't mine. I questioned my girlfriend about the baby not being mine. She broke down and started crying. She went into this grand story about how the guy that pulled the gun on me weeks ago had raped her. I knew it was a lie.

However, she was willing to take her story to the fullest. She wanted me to take her to the police station so that she could file criminal charges on him. I knew immediately that the guy didn't rape her and I wasn't willing to have a bogus rape charge placed on him for something I know he very well he didn't do. Even if he did pull a gun on me a couple of weeks earlier. That day, I got in my car and left, I never saw here again.

At this time, I was staying with my grandmother because my mother kicked me out the house. One night while I was on the phone with my new girlfriend, my stepfather asked me to get off the telephone and take out the trash. I refused. We had a few words and it almost ensued into something physical. My mother stepped in and had to separate the two of us. After things subsided, my mother asked me to leave.

Only 3 out of 100 Black males entering kindergarten will graduate from college. Every 5 seconds during the school day, a Black public-school student is suspended. Every 46 seconds during the school day, a Black high school student drops out.

Every minute, a Black child is arrested and a Black baby is born to an unmarried mother. Every 3 minutes, a Black child is born into poverty. Every hour, a Black child dies. Every 4 hours, a Black child or youth under 20 dies from an accident, and every 5 hours, a Black youth is a homicide victim. Every day, a Black young person under 25 dies from HIV infection and a Black child or youth under 20 commits suicide.

My first day at the private high school was a very different. I noticed immediately that there was only about ten black students. Of these ten black students, eight were athletes. This school was so different from the public schools I attended in the past. I had to attend mass every day. At my other school, I received free lunch. Here I had to buy all my meals. Money was very limited; my grandmother was on a fixed income.

In the beginning, I would just sit in the cafeteria with my friends and didn't eat. Some days, I had a little money, but most days I was hungry. One day as I was walking through the lunch line with a friend, I decided to take a chicken sandwich. I shoved it in my pocket and walked through the checkout line as if nothing had happened. I continued taking food for weeks until one of the lunchroom workers saw me.

She pulled me to the side and advised me that they were fully aware of what I was doing. She told me that they had a lot of extra food left over and if I was hungry to just ask and not steal it.

Academics by far was the most challenging thing at this new school. Coming from a public school, with a learning disability, being in special education, having repeated two grades, and probably reading on a fifth-grade level, this was truly going to be a challenge. Catholic High had a policy in place for athletes.

Athletes had to attend mandatory 30-minute tutoring after school called tutorials. My teachers went out of their way to work with me. They tried their best to bring me up to speed with the other students.

That year the basketball team instantly turned it around. The season before I arrived at Catholic High, they were 2-22, this season we went 18-12. Not long after basketball season, I received a page to come to the office. After speaking with the principal, he informed me that I couldn't' return to school until I brought my grandmother back with me. The next day my mother and I sat in his office. He stated that my tuition had not been paid the entire school year. I explained that it was my understanding that I didn't have to pay any tuition. It was made very clear from the first day that my family couldn't afford to pay for me to attend this school.

The principal informed me and my grandmother that I could no longer attend Catholic High School. The principal gave me my transcripts and told me that the best thing would be for me to go and enroll in another high school. I went home a little rejected that day. I began to think, I am seventeen and reading on a 5th grade level; I decided to just forgo any more schooling and I dropped out. Dropping out wasn't anything new in my family. My mom dropped out. My real dad dropped out. My brother was put out of school and my sister dropped out.

A 2006 study by The Manhattan Institute surveyed 100 of the largest school districts in the United States and found that only 48 percent of African-American males earned a diploma—that's 11 percent less than African-American females. More troubling is the research that shows on an average day, one and four Black males who drop out of high school will end up incarcerated. High rates of placement in special education classes and disproportionate use of suspension and expulsion only exacerbate the problem. The graduation numbers for Black males are dismal, chilling, and undeniably pathetic.

The nation graduates only 47% of Black males who enter the 9th grade. Black males face an upheaval educational battle: their graduation statistics are sobering across America.

My grandmother pleaded with me on several attempts to go back to school but I just didn't feel that there was any hope in me going back. When I told my mother that I had dropped out, she just looked at me and didn't have any comments.

Today's young people are partners, parents, workers, citizens of tomorrow. Unless they master the skills required to manage their own emotions, treat others with respect, negotiate points of disagreement and conflict, build their capacity for productive work, and work cooperatively with others, America's society as a whole will suffer.

WHY?

WHY IS THIS IMPORTANT?

Why did you start teaching? Remembering why you started teaching is very important. There are going to be ups and downs, trials and tribulations, and times when you get annoyed and feel like walking away from it all. I suggest that when you begin to feel fed up with teaching, to sit down in a quiet place and remember why did I start teaching and hopefully this will help you overcome all the challenges that come with teaching at-risk kids.

Right Motives, Wrong Methods

One Million Students

WHY IS THIS IMPORTANT?

Each year in America over one million students' drop-out annually. Either you as an educator are part of the problem, or part of the solution. I challenge educators to really do a self-check and ask yourself if you are doing what it takes to help at-risk students succeed. I understand that its challenging, but in many cases, educators may be the only constructive person that many at-risk students see on a day to day basis.

Right Motives, Wrong Methods

Stop Taking "IT" Personal

WHY IS THIS IMPORTANT?

Too often educators take it personal (get into their feelings) when students disrespect them. I understand that its challenging to avoid getting aggravated when students disrespect you. In most cases, students really don't have a personal problem with you as an educator. They are furious at life. Students who have been trodden by life, often walk around looking for confrontations, physically or verbally. Therefore, when a student seemingly feels disrespected, they will react accordingly. The irony is that in most cases they will respond like that with whomever they feel disrespected them. It's not you, educators, its life that has pissed them off. STOP TAKING IT PERSONAL!

Right Motives, Wrong Methods

Breaking the Rules!

WHY IS THIS IMPORTANT?

Ms. Gaston was my 6th grade teacher and would eventually become one of my favorite teaches. One day during a dreadful thunder storm; Ms. Gaston pulled up in her grey Honda Accord as my siblings and I were walking home. She rolled her window down and asked if we needed a ride home? I said no, but she insisted. We loaded in her car and she drove us home. Anyone in education understands that this is prohibited. Anything could've happened, anything could've been said to have happen, and this could have perhaps cost Ms. Gaston her job. From that day, Ms. Gaston never had another issue in class with me. She earned my respect. Sometimes you may have to break the rules, to make the connections.

Right Motives, Wrong Methods

Stop Humiliating Students!

WHY IS THIS IMPORTANT?

Humiliation is never ok, every student in school deserves the right to feel emotionally safe from embarrassment and humiliation by educators. Today's students are **BIG** on respect. The moment they feel disrespected they are going to react negatively especially if they have an audience of peers watching.

Right Motives, Wrong Methods

Do You Really
Know Your Students?

WHY IS THIS IMPORTANT?

Students have numerous things going on outside of your classroom/school. As an educator have you ever taken the time to ask one of your students about their personal issues? When they talk do you listen or just try to push your opinions on them?

Right Motives, Wrong Methods

Empathy vs Sympathy

WHY IS THIS IMPORTANT?

Empathy is often confused with pity, sympathy, and compassion, which are each reaction to the plight of students. Having pity on students is less engaging than empathy, sympathy, or compassion. There is a fine line between sympathy and empathy. Learning the difference can play a huge role in the relationship with your at-risk students. Sympathy is about sharing. It directs attention to how "you" feel. Empathy is about "listening." It tells your student you understand. Sympathy is an expression of how you feel in response to someone else's experience or feelings. Empathy has nothing to do with how you feel; it's about understanding how the other feels given their circumstance.

Right Motives, Wrong Methods

At-Risk students don't care about your curriculum/lesson plan, until they know that you care about their situations outside of your classroom!

WHY IS THIS IMPORTANT?

As educators, you have to understand that students experience all types of situations outside of your class. These situations affect how students react and function during the school day. Until you care about their situation outside of your class, they will not care about your curriculum/lesion plan inside the classroom.

Right Motives, Wrong Methods

Super Spiritual

WHY IS THIS IMPORTANT?

Yeah, I said it, most students become frustrated with educators who are always preaching Jesus, Jesus, Jesus, at them. Most students just desire an adult who can converse with them about real life and not at them about super spiritual things they truly don't understand. I am not saying your religion is a bad thing, I am saying have some balance when it comes to kids.

Right Motives, Wrong Methods

Parental Involvement

WHY IS THIS IMPORTANT?

Try not to get frustrated when your parental involvement is not where you would like for it to be. Educators and principals have to find innovative techniques to get at-risk parents involved and motivated. My wife, a third-grade teacher in Alabama places her personal cellphone number in her weekly newsletter. She understands that most of her parents will text her before they call or come to the school. I am not telling you to do the same but again you have to get creative when you deal with at-risk parents.

Right Motives, Wrong Methods

Surrogates

WHY IS THIS IMPORTANT?

Today schools as well as educators are being forced to act as "surrogate" families because some parents struggle to bring their kids up properly. I have heard teachers say to student's "I am not your mother," however, the reality is that if a student begins to act as if you are a parent, it's a complement. Which should make it very easy to generate a relationship with that student.

Right Motives, Wrong Methods

At-Risk Parents

WHY IS THIS IMPORTANT?

I totally understand that some of your parent's may make you want to pull your hair out by its roots. However, as ghetto, or as ignorant as a parent may seem. You can never disrespect a student's parent in front of the student. The moment you do, that student will lose the little respect he or she has for you as an educator. I recommend pulling the parent in a room away from the student and then have a real adult conversation with him or her. But never in front of the student.

Special Education

WHY IS THIS IMPORTANT?

Most students view Special Education as negative and uncool. As a former special education student, I can honestly say I would have rather been suspended then sit in a Special Education class.

Right Motives, Wrong Methods

At-Risk Kids

WHY IS THIS IMPORTANT?

Not all students that come from the inner cities in America are gangbangers and/or drug dealers. Not all parents that live in impoverish areas lack the motivation to become involved in their kid's education. Motivating parents can be frustrating. However, understanding that your parents are most likely products of an environment where their parents did the same will help you better understand how to deal with them.

Right Motives, Wrong Methods

"Pedagogy of Poverty"

WHY IS THIS IMPORTANT?

Pedagogy of poverty originates through a teachers' desire for control, in the conception of children as having no innate desire to learn, in the belief of student freedom as synonymous to permissiveness, in the limited understanding of pedagogical technique, and in the low expectations of minorities and the poor.

Right Motives, Wrong Methods

Being too Hard
on Yourself

WHY IS THIS IMPORTANT?

Teaching is difficult enough without the additional challenge of mental anguish over slip-ups, mistakes, and imperfections. No teacher perfect. Even the most decorated and experience teachers make poor decisions every so often. It's not a mistake if you learn from it.

Right Motives, Wrong Methods

Teacher Clicks

WHY IS THIS IMPORTANT?

This pitfall is an equal opportunity offender for both new and veteran teachers. Like all workplaces, the school campus can be rife with squabbles, grudges, backstabbing, and vendettas. It's a slippery slope if you agree to listen to gossip because, before you know it, you'll be taking sides and immersing yourself in between warring factions. The political fallout can be brutal. Better to just keep your interactions friendly and neutral, while focusing intently on the work with your students. Avoid politics at all costs and your teaching career will thrive!

Teacher's Pride

WHY IS THIS IMPORTANT?

Teachers can be a proud bunch. Your job requires superhuman skills, so you often strive to appear as superheroes who can handle any problem that comes your way. But that simply can't be the case. Don't be afraid to appear vulnerable, admit mistakes, and ask your colleagues or administrators for assistance. Look around your school and you will see centuries of teaching experience represented by your fellow teachers. More often than not, these professionals are generous with their time and advice. Ask for help and you just might discover that you're not as alone as you thought you were.

Right Motives, Wrong Methods

Buddies with Students

WHY IS THIS IMPORTANT?

Inexperienced and sometimes experienced teachers often fall into the trap of wanting their students to like them above all else. Instead, focus on earning your students' respect, admiration, and appreciation. Once you realize that your students will respect you more when you are tough and fair with them, you'll be on the right track.

Right Motives, Wrong Methods

Don't Get Stuck in A Singular Mode of Teaching

WHY IS THIS IMPORTANT?

Change things up on your students. Often times teachers get caught up in doing things one way. Teachers are as much creatures of habit as anyone else. When things become boring and too predictable, discipline problems are undoubtedly going to become an issue.

Be Consistent in Expectations and Discipline

WHY IS THIS IMPORTANT?

Consistent execution of the rules helps students to maintain the respect fostered in the classroom. Once these rules are in place, I feel the most vital piece of classroom management is developing relationships of trust and equality. If this is the ultimate goal of a student-teacher relationship, real learning can take place.

Right Motives, Wrong Methods

Make Your Expectations Clear from the Get-Go

WHY IS THIS IMPORTANT?

Take the time to teach expectations, and reteach them as needed. This may feel like you are wasting time that could be spent on curriculum, but when you add up the time it would take to do a menial task throughout your semester or year, you are actually adding time spent on instruction.

Right Motives, Wrong Methods

Try to Look at Things From Your Students' Perspective and be Empathetic

WHY IS THIS IMPORTANT?

I strongly, firmly believe that if teachers do not wear their students' shoes when necessary, they are not doing their job well. This is especially true when dealing with at risk students... teachers have to be extremely careful about what they say and how they say what they need to.

Right Motives, Wrong Methods

Greeting Your Students
At The Door

WHY IS THIS IMPORTANT?

Greeting your students at the door means nothing if you're not doing it to develop relationships with them day in and day out. Make sure you're not just greeting them as a formality.

Right Motives, Wrong Methods

Confronting Misbehaving Students

WHY IS THIS IMPORTANT?

Confrontations misbehaving students in front of classmates almost always become escalated. I would recommend asking the student to step out of the classroom.

Right Motives, Wrong Methods

Pick Your Rules Wisely, More Rules Doesn't Always Equate to Better Behavior!

WHY IS THIS IMPORTANT?

An environment that is dictated by too many rules is rigid, cold and likely to create an atmosphere of rebellion... Rules and routines are an excellent way to communicate your behavioral expectations, but not the way to completely manage your classroom.

Right Motives, Wrong Methods

"Be Real"

WHY IS THIS IMPORTANT?

Educators should be "Real," students can smell fake from a mile away.

Right Motives, Wrong Methods

"Be Respectful"

WHY IS THIS IMPORTANT?

Educators should be "Respectful," your students will never respond the way you desire, if you approach them disrespectfully. This is a different generation of kids and they live by a different set of rules. They believe that a teacher should respect them first, and then they'll think about respecting you later. Respect is everything, if you feel that's all you have.

Right Motives, Wrong Methods

"Make it Relevant"

WHY IS THIS IMPORTANT?

Educators should attempt to make the information they teach "Relevant." Student's desire to know, how is this information going to help me in the future? If they fail to see the connection, they may not be intrigued to learn it.

Right Motives, Wrong Methods

"Develop Relationships"

WHY IS THIS IMPORTANT?

Relationships are the foundation for motivating at-risk students and getting them motivated to complete work assignments. Please note that **relationships are not formed overnight.** They take time, but once you develop the relationship with a student, so much more time can be devoted to teaching.

Right Motives, Wrong Methods

PLEASE DON'T!

WHY IS THIS IMPORTANT?

Please don't tell another educator that a certain student is coming next year and that you need to watch out for him or her. He or She may be the very teacher that can touch his heart and change his life.

Right Motives, Wrong Methods

PLEASE DON'T!

WHY IS THIS IMPORTANT?

Please don't place a sibling in a box. Please don't put a student's brother or sister in a box based off of their sibling's behavior. That's not fair to the brother or sister.

Right Motives, Wrong Methods

PLEASE DON'T!

WHY IS THIS IMPORTANT?

Please don't tell a student "I got mine," I understand that students will push you to the edge, but telling a student that will only push a student further away and make them feel that you really don't care.

Right Motives, Wrong Methods

PLEASE DON'T!

WHY IS THIS IMPORTANT?

Please don't tell students that "I am just here to get a pay check." Conveys YOU REALLY DON'T CARE!!!! I have never met an educator that went into education because they wanted to become a millionaire. Most educators go into education to help students.

Right Motives, Wrong Methods

PLEASE DON'T!

WHY IS THIS IMPORTANT?

Please don't tell students that "I am just here to get a paycheck." Conveys YOU REALLY DON'T CARE!!!! I have never met an educator that went into education because they wanted to become a millionaire. Most educators go into education to help students.

Right Motives, Wrong Methods

Teacher at the beginning of the school year

Teacher at the end of the school year

WHY IS THIS IMPORTANT?

If teaching was easy, everyone would be doing it!!!! You are the real HERO!!! Thanks for all that you do! Please remember that an educator just like you help save my life.

Right Motives, Wrong Methods

PLEASE DON'T!

WHY IS THIS IMPORTANT?

Educators please try not to treat your teacher assistants/paraprofessionals like they are beneath you. If they are able to form valuable relationships with hard to reach students. Please just ask him or her for help. You guys are a team and the educational system needs all hands-on deck working together to help these at-risk students.

Right Motives, Wrong Methods

Home Life

WHY IS THIS IMPORTANT?

The home environment shapes the initial attitudes that students hold toward learning. In a home where curiosity, questions, and exploration are encouraged, kids are given the message that education is worthwhile and personally satisfying.

Right Motives, Wrong Methods

PLEASE DON'T!

WHY IS THIS IMPORTANT?

Educators please try not to treat your teacher assistants/paraprofessionals like they are beneath you. If they are able to form valuable relationships with hard to reach students. Please just ask him or her for help. You guys are a team and the educational system needs all hands-on deck working together to help these at-risk students.

Right Motives, Wrong Methods

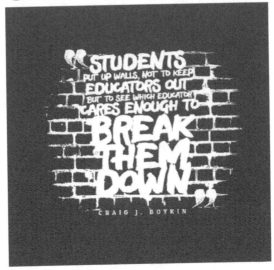

WHY IS THIS IMPORTANT?

Breaking down walls take time. You have to be patient with kids.

Right Motives, Wrong Methods

Students Home Environment

WHY IS THIS IMPORTANT?

When you grow up in an environment where all you hear is words such as the "F" word, and the "B" word. It tends to become the norm. YOU cannot take it personal if a student drops the "B" word on you. It may be the only way they know how to communicate.

Right Motives, Wrong Methods

Students Home Environment

WHY IS THIS IMPORTANT?

When you grow up in an environment where all you hear is words such as the "F" word, and the "B" word. It tends to become the norm. YOU cannot take it personal if a student drops the "B" word on you. It may be the only way they know how to communicate.

Right Motives, Wrong Methods

What causes a lack of student motivation?

WHY IS THIS IMPORTANT?

Many students are too adsorbed in "Now" thinking and not enough "Future" thinking. They do not look ahead into the future, which is why many doesn't see any value in education.

Right Motives, Wrong Methods

What causes a lack of student motivation?

WHY IS THIS IMPORTANT?

Educators not working together is a serious problem in America! America has over a million students annually dropping out. We need all educators working collectively together. I am not asking you to become bff's (best friends forever), but we do need educators that are willing to work together.

Right Motives, Wrong Methods

What causes a lack of student motivation?

WHY IS THIS IMPORTANT?

Educators and Parents not on the SAME PAGE! If you have a problem with a student's parent, never disrespect that parent in front of the student. The moment you do the student will lose all respect that he or she had for you.

Right Motives, Wrong Methods

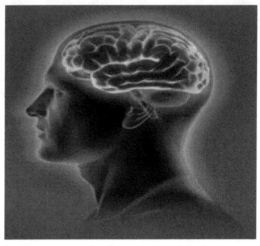

WHY IS THIS IMPORTANT?

The human brain has two modes, either it will focus on growing/evolving one's life, or the brain will focus on survival, its challenging for the brain to try to do both simultaneously. When a student has some hazardous situations at home it's almost impossible for them to focus on learning. The brain was also created to learn and not unlearn. All the bad habits students learn at home become ingrained in their brains as normal. It's not impossible to rid these habits, but it will be hard.

Right Motives, Wrong Methods

Respect

WHY IS THIS IMPORTANT?

This Generation of students are unlike any before. This generation demands to be respected by educators first, then and only then will they think about respecting you. I am not saying this is right, but it is the way things are.

Right Motives, Wrong Methods

Education

WHY IS THIS IMPORTANT?

Many at-risk students don't consider education as a way out of their current situation. It's my experience that they gravitate towards Rapping, selling drugs, and sports.

Right Motives, Wrong Methods

WHY IS THIS IMPORTANT?

Educators have to avoid profiling students because they don't look like what we think they should look like. If you have never sat down and had a discussion with those students, then you don't have the right to pre-judge them. I often say, "you're not going to walk through hell and come out snow white."

Right Motives, Wrong Methods

WHY IS THIS IMPORTANT?

A teacher had a student that would come to school each morning and place his head on his desk and go to sleep. Instead of sending the student to the office she decided to ask him why was he so sleepy every morning? The student replied, "I don't know Mrs. Smith, but every time my daddy smokes those cigarettes (marijuana) in the car on the way to school, I get really sleepy." Ask yourself, what would you have done if this had happened in your class. FYI, she let the young man sleep it off and later spoke with his parents.

Right Motives, Wrong Methods

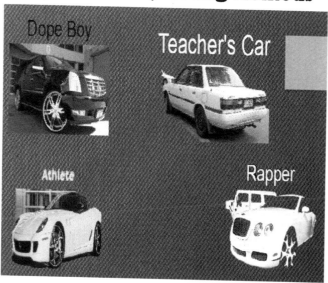

WHY IS THIS IMPORTANT?

The problem is that many at-risk students view education as non-profitable. Therefore, they will only give minimal effect and put maximum effect towards things they believe can change their circumstances such as rapping, sports, and unfortunately selling drugs.

Right Motives, Wrong Methods

WHY IS THIS IMPORTANT?

Be careful not to reward students by sending them to their "superhero" teacher. In school, I would often get into trouble on purpose in class because I didn't like teacher "A" and I loved teacher "B." If you're not careful as an educator you will end up transferring all your power to the "superhero" teacher.

Right Motives, Wrong Methods

WHY IS THIS IMPORTANT?

I had a teacher that handed me a graded test paper with no grade, it only had a smiley face on it. I asked her what was my grade? She replied, "don't worry about that Craig, I am proud that you did your very best." Some of your student's experience low self-esteem and giving them a paper with an "F" only hurts their already damaged self-esteem.

Right Motives, Wrong Methods

Perfection vs Progress

WHY IS THIS IMPORTANT?

It is very important that educators don't get caught up in trying to perfect at-risk student and miss when a student shows progress. Praise the small things. If a student misses school often and you notice that. I need you to also notice when he or she has not missed a day in weeks and acknowledge that. If he or she missed three or four days in a single week you would point that out. So, address when the students shows a little progress. The student will appreciate you noticing.

Right Motives, Wrong Methods

WHY IS THIS IMPORTANT?

Remember it's easier to development healthy relationships with challenging/at risk students while they are in another teacher's classroom/grade. It allows you to be the "good" cop so to speak and let the other teacher be the "bad" cop. By the time the student reaches your grade/classroom the ground work has already been laid and it makes your life a lot easier.

Right Motives, Wrong Methods

WHY IS THIS IMPORTANT?

It's hard to sit in class and focus on learning when you're hungry. I understand that it's not your responsible as an educator to make sure that students have something eat. However, I am simply asking that you acknowledge that it is a struggle to concentrate when you're hungry. FYI, providing snacks may very well be what opens the door for communication between the two of you and leads to a great relationship.

Right Motives, Wrong Methods

First Impressions:

A teacher from South Carolina approached me after a presentation to inquire about something that had happen between he and a student. This was his first year at this school (100% free lunch). He came from a rural school. After every class, teachers would stand in the hallway to monitor the students. One day during the first week of school, he noticed a black male walking down the hall with his pants sagging. He approached the young man and insisted that he pull his pants up immediately. The student looked at the teacher and shot him a bird and told him to go "F" himself and walked off. The teacher asked me "what did I do wrong?" I laughed, I asked him has he ever spoken to the young man before that day? He replied, no. I said that's why. To the young man, he doesn't know you. Even if you are a teacher, walking up to him and demanding that he pull his pants up was very disrespectful. I would have attempted to get to know him before demanding something like pulling up his pants.

Right Motives, Wrong Methods

WHY IS THIS IMPORTANT?

Educators should always attempt to apologize to students when they are wrong. It's amazing to me that educators don't feel they need to apologize to students when they make a mistake. Apologizing opens the door to form relationships with students.

Right Motives, Wrong Methods

WHY IS THIS IMPORTANT?

Educators should seek first to understand, then to be understood. It will help tremendously if you wouldn't be so quick to jump to conclusions about your students. Don't Assume, ask!

Right Motives, Wrong Methods

WHY IS THIS IMPORTANT?

If you don't like a student, you don't have let them know it!!! I hear teachers all the time expressing their dislike for a particular student. Remember what I said earlier in this book, you can't make it personal with students.

Right Motives, Wrong Methods

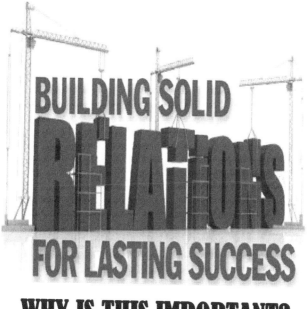

WHY IS THIS IMPORTANT?

Trust is an essential foundation on which to build a relationship. If you tell a student that you're going to do something, do it. Trust is hard to get, but easily lost.

Right Motives, Wrong Methods

WHY IS THIS IMPORTANT?

Make your actions match your words. If you say you're going to do something, do it. Breaking your word is one of the fastest ways to lose students gained trust.

Right Motives, Wrong Methods

WHY IS THIS IMPORTANT?

Be open to feedback. It puzzles me when educators don't ask for feedback from their students. Then it dawned on me, students are going to be completely honesty and teachers may not want to hear that their teaching style sucks!!! But remember you cannot grow if you don't receive feedback.

Right Motives, Wrong Methods

WHY IS THIS IMPORTANT?

Educators have to be vulnerable with students. Students need to see and know that educators are human. Vulnerability is a significant feature of a lasting relationship.

Right Motives, Wrong Methods

WHY IS THIS IMPORTANT?

Educators should be committed to the challenge. Building relationships with at-risk students will take 100% commitment from you.

Right Motives, Wrong Methods

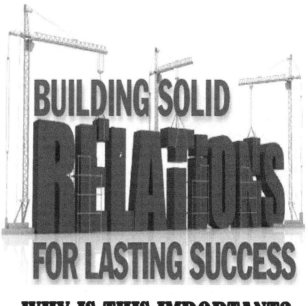

WHY IS THIS IMPORTANT?

The mediocre teacher tells. The good teacher explains. The superior teacher demonstrates. The great teacher inspires.

Right Motives, Wrong Methods

WHY IS THIS IMPORTANT?

"If kids come to us from strong, healthy functioning families, it makes our job easier. If they do not come to us from strong, healthy, functioning families, it makes our job more important." -Barbara Colorose

Right Motives, Wrong Methods

WHY IS THIS IMPORTANT?

"We are now at a point where we must educate our children in what no one knew yesterday, and prepare our schools for what no one knows yet." Margaret Mead

Right Motives, Wrong Methods

WHY IS THIS IMPORTANT?

Jesus was said to be the best inspirational speaker to ever walk planet earth. As great as he was he couldn't save everyone. As educators, it's a naïve approach to believe that you can save every student that walks into your classroom. Your job as an educator is to give 100% of yourself to your students and if they still fall through the cracks you can rest at night knowing you did your best.

Right Motives, Wrong Methods

WHY IS THIS IMPORTANT?

Students should be highly motivated and functioning in the sky-blue section of self-actualized, however when the lower area of Maslow's chart are broken/missing it makes it that much more difficult to desire to grow.

Right Motives, Wrong Methods

WHY IS THIS IMPORTANT?

Are you that one teacher? Most adults will agree that they can point back to one teacher that in some way changed their life. For me it was Jennifer Gaston, Mrs. Gaston was the very first educator that told me I could become whatever I wanted to in life. She expressed her understanding of my difficult circumstances, but urged me not to allow them to dictate my future.

Right Motives, Wrong Methods

WHY IS THIS IMPORTANT?

At-risk students are more concerned about someone helping them then the race of the educator. Educators always come up to me and say, "I can't relate to my children of color" and my response to them is always the same. If you build the relationship the student can careless what your race is. They understand that you have their best interest at heart.

Right Motives, Wrong Methods

Job or Calling

WHY IS THIS IMPORTANT?

You have to do some soul-searching educators. Humans tend to quit jobs when the going gets tough. As for a calling, it's something that most humans tend to stick with even in the face of adversity because there is something on the inside of them that will not allow them to sleep if they are not doing it. **Is teaching a JOB or why you were created?**

Conclusion

There is no longer a need for predictions, hand-wringing, or apprehension about losing a generation of young people. It is severely too late. In education, employment readiness, economics, incarceration, health, housing, and parenting, we have lost a generation of young people.

The only question that remains is, "Will we "America" lose the next two or three generations, or possibly every generation of black's hereafter to the streets, negative media, gangs, drugs, poor education, unemployment, father absence, crime, violence, lack of parenting and death?"

Literacy levels amongst minorities are lower on average than they should be. Many scholars have written on the subject, attempting to find a reason for and a solution to the problem. There is some confusion over where the source of the problem lies. For example, some believe that an improvement in the curriculum will solve much of the problem. However, the problem is more likely due to a lack of motivation amongst minority students to work hard in school. Engaging minorities so that they are interested in education is a daunting task, but it is an important issue that must be addressed. Achieving success outside of dangerous careers in organized crime is nearly impossible without a solid academic foundation.

My grandmother would always say to me that there is more than one way to skin a cat. Piggybacking off of that old saying, I believe that there is more than one way to help struggling at-risk youth in the classroom. When educators attempt to use the same old techniques with children today that they used 20 years ago, it can become frustrating for students as well as educators.

"One of the great liabilities of history is that all too many people fail to remain awake through great periods of social change. Every society has its protectors of status quo and its fraternities of the indifferent who are notorious for sleeping through revolutions. Today, our very survival depends on our ability to stay awake, to adjust to new ideas, to remain vigilant and to face the challenge of change." Rev. Dr. Martin Luther King, Jr.

Teachers throughout America are frustrated with the day-to-day struggles of trying to teach in urban schools and not understanding why so many kids are just not motivated to do well. This book is an attempt to help educators better understand the mind-set of their at-risk students and develop supportive strategies to assist the students as they become more academically focused and motivated.

Personally, I struggled with education from kindergarten until I dropped out in the 10th grade. Growing up, I dealt with so many factors outside of classroom, it was difficult to focus on what teachers were trying to teach. There were a number of issues present during my childhood such as my mother was addicted to drugs, my father was not present, I was illiterate, I was in special education because I had a learning disability, along with countless of issues. Day in and day out, I sat in classrooms feeling as if no one really understood what I was going through.

Nor did it feel as if they really cared. Therefore, the frustration and resentment began to fester, and I began to hate education, my teachers, and even my life. I took it personally when teachers would ask me to read or try to get me to do my schoolwork. In many cases, I reacted with anger and/or defiance, which resulted in frequent suspension.

For at at-risk students, trying to navigate school as well as life can be difficult. As I present at different schools, conferences, workshops, etc., the question remains the same. "Craig what can I do to make a difference in my student's life?"

I hear teacher after teacher expressing how much potential their students have, but those students are distracted by so many things outside of school. I often express educators that in most cases, if we fail to educate these at-risk students, their next step could be incarceration or the cemetery. According to Tony Miller, "Partnering for Education Reform." U.S. Department of Education, every year, over 1.2 million students drop out of high school in the United States alone. That's every 26 seconds or 7,000 a day.

It is my desire that superintendents, administrators, teachers, counselors, special education coordinators, and anyone who works with at-risk students can use this book as a tool to improve techniques for how to deal with at-risk students. In this manuscript, you will encounter a unique dose of my first-hand account/ experiences being an at-risk student, coupled with relevant research.

The least-experienced, least classroom-trained teachers are often assigned to the most difficult schools. They enter the field with the expectation that they have been adequately prepared by the schools of education with the skills they need and they haven't received. They are leaving the field faster than colleges can prepare them. The teacher "dropout rate" is higher than the student dropout rate. Forty-six percent of teachers leave the field within five years. When asked why they leave, a majority state that they haven't been properly prepared, have had increased demands placed on them because of high-stakes testing, and are not getting adequate support from their supervisors in dealing with classroom discipline.

There is often a clash between the family values and those of the school. Frequently, their parents have dropped out of school themselves. The students come from families from low socio-economic backgrounds, where there are many other children. Older children often have to go to work in order to supply the family with much-needed funds for basic family needs or need to stay home to take care of younger siblings so that their parents can work.

Several factors contribute to students lack of motivation. The modern entertainment media provides too many distractions. Entertainment takes on a higher priority than education. They have a physical problem, such as vision or hearing problems, and give up. Students with significant learning disabilities who have not received help, are discouraged, and have given up. They become convinced that they cannot do the work. "So why even try?" Negative peer influences are too great. "I don't want to be a nerd or teacher's pet." Parents and other family adults are not involved enough to instill the basis of self-motivation.

Today, often both parents hold jobs outside the home. Parents may be addicted to drugs. These are nuclear families, and there are no other adults to provide loving guidance, wisdom, and motivation. These children do not see the relevance of the school material in their lives. They don't see school as providing any benefit to them. The teachers are not taking sufficient steps to motivate. These students are too adsorbed in "now" thinking and not enough "future" thinking. They do not look ahead into the future.

RIGHT MOTIVES, WRONG METHODS
CRAIG J. BOYKIN

Imagine the absolute worse student you have ever encountered during you educational career. That was Craig!

Overcame Enormous Odds

Mother On Drugs, Absent Father, Learning Disability, Special Educatio Student, Repeated 3rd & 5th Grade, High School Dropout, Shot By A Gan Member At Age 18.

Today, Craig J. Boykin is a renowned keynote speaker, author, communit activist, and mentor. Craig has devoted his life to creating lasting chang for those who desire it; Craig has risen to national stage by delivering h inspirational message which tells people how to shake off mediocrity and liv up to their greatness. It is a message Craig has learned from his own life an one he is helping others apply to their lives. Craig is one of the nation's leadin authorities in understanding and stimulating human potential, utilizing powerful delivery and newly emerging insights to teach, inspire and channe people to new levels of achievement.

Craig is one of the nation's leading authoritie in understanding and stimulating huma potential, utilizing a powerful delivery and newl emerging insights to teach, inspire and channe people to new levels of achievement. Craig' personal mission in life is to provide hope t individuals who feel that their current situatio is hopeless. Craig travels the country presentin his seminar, "Make Life Count." Craig publishe his first book in 2013 entitled, "My Life, You Inspiration" and has been featured on TBN, wor various awards, and his story has been shared i many inspirational and motivational magazines.

$19.95
ISBN 978-0-692-47860-8
51995>

9 780692 478608

A Gift of Grace

By Noelle Sellers